THE
UNCOMMON
MINISTER

**Wisdom Keys
For A Ministry
Of Excellence
And Greatness**

VOLUME **2**

MIKE MURDOCK

TABLE OF CONTENTS

1 CREATE THE HABIT OF LISTENING TO
   SCRIPTURE TAPES DAILY.   3

2 INSIST ON ACCURACY IN YOUR PREACHING.   6

3 LEARN FROM THE UNHAPPY VOICES
   AROUND YOU.   9

4 NEVER DISCUSS IN THE PULPIT ANYTHING
   YOU WANT OTHERS TO FORGET.   13

5 IDENTIFY CONTENTIOUS PEOPLE INVOLVED
   IN YOUR MINISTRY.   17

6 SECURE THE BEST OFFICE EQUIPMENT
   POSSIBLE FOR YOUR MINISTRY.   21

7 VALUE THE VOWS OF YOUR PEOPLE.   24

Unless otherwise indicated, all Scripture quotations are taken from the King James Version of the Bible.

The Uncommon Minister, Volume 2
Copyright © 1999 by Mike Murdock
ISBN 1-56394-101-5

Published by The Wisdom Center
P. O. Box 99 • Denton, Texas 76202

To avoid the burdensome verbage of him/her; his, hers throughout this book, the simple reference to all of mankind, male or female, is simply "he" or "him."

≈ 1 ≈

CREATE THE HABIT OF LISTENING TO SCRIPTURE TAPES DAILY.

Listening is different than reading.

You cannot read and do other things at the same time. Reading requires total *focus.* You have to move away from everything else that you are doing.

However, listening can begin the moment you awaken. This is powerful.

While you are washing your face, *you can receive the words of Jesus* into your spirit.

While you are shaving, taking a bath or making up your bed, you can receive His words into the soil of your mind. Most of us take an hour or so to birth our day. That is 60 minutes that the holy words of God could be *washing your mind.*

His Word *cleanses.* (See John 15:3.)

His Word *energizes.* (Read Psalm 119:149,156.)

His Word is *life.* (Read John 6:63.)

His Word *purges and purifies.* (See Psalm 119:9.)

His Word *corrects you.* (See 2 Timothy 3:16.)

His Word *warns.* (See Psalm 119:11.)

His Word *brings peace.* (Read Psalm 119:165.)

His Word *births an invisible joy* that cannot be explained by anyone. (Read John 15:11.)

Here's what has happened in my own life. Sometimes, I become so busy I delay taking my Bible and reading quietly in my Secret Place. I "explain" to the Lord that I will meet with Him later "when I can really concentrate and not be distracted by anything else." (This procrastination has cost me dearly.)

Listening to Scriptures on cassette tapes solves that problem *immediately*. Satan can throw many things at you, but the Word of God is *still washing* your mind, because of your *daily* habit of listening.

Listening is not a substitution for reading. You need *both*.

▶ Reading affects your *thinking*.
▶ Listening affects your *feelings*.
▶ Reading affects your *mind*.
▶ Listening influences your *emotions*.

His Word always creates marvelous results, regardless of how you receive it into your spirit. I have found that keeping tapes with me in motel rooms, next to my bed, and in my automobile really influences me.

Keep tapes in your car. They will discourage boring conversationalists who talk about trivia and other unimportant things. Also, it makes it possible to hear His Word separate from the clutter of business and home chores.

Keep tapes next to your bed. Sometimes, when I'm having difficulty sleeping, I will punch "play" on my cassette recorder and listen to the Scriptures. Words cannot describe how instantly an atmosphere and climate can change in your bedroom when the Word of God fills up every corner!

Keep tapes on your desk at your church. Using your headphones, you will always find an opportunity to receive His Word into your spirit.

> ► *Your ministry will change* in direct proportion to the Words you are hearing from Him.
>
> ► *Your personal joy* will be proportionate to the Words you are hearing from Him.
>
> ► *Your people will change* proportionate to the passion you birth in them for the Word of God.

Nobody else can do this for you. You must pursue the Word of God for *yourself. Today.*

Somebody has said that it takes 56 hours to read the entire Bible through. Whatever it takes, do it. Do it today. Concentrate on developing this habit.

His Word is the most important thing you will hear today.

It will change you and your ministry forever.

Create The Habit Of Listening To Tapes Daily.

It is One of the Secrets of The Uncommon Minister.

∼ 2 ∼

Insist On Accuracy In Your Preaching.

Accuracy really does matter.

Moses built the tabernacle. But the Golden Key was his accuracy in obedience to the pattern God gave him.

Noah built the ark. But the Golden Key was building it *accurately*, according to the command.

Solomon built the temple. But the important ingredient was building it *according to the pattern* that the Holy Spirit gave to David and him.

The Pharisees prayed. But their prayers were worthless. You see, it is not enough to simply pray. You must pray according to the will of God. The Pharisees fasted. But Jesus revealed a different set of instructions regarding the power of fasting. Attitude was everything.

The Uncommon Minister must invest the time and effort to be accurate every time he ministers.

Several years ago, a real tragedy occurred for a well-known ministry. The young man carried a real anointing on his ministry. He was expressive. Fiery. Opinionated. Purposeful. One day, he threw out some so-called facts and illustrations that were later proven libelous. He was sued for a huge amount of money. Though a settlement out of court might have occurred, it created terrible distractions for himself, his staff, and his ministry. He lost many partners who did not really understand the warfare against him. His attention to *accuracy* would have prevented this tragic interruption and distraction in his ministry. I was once told that a well-known comedian had died. I used it for an illustration that night in the message only to find out later my source was completely wrong. He was still alive! It made me look like a fool and even sowed Seeds of doubt about the rest of my information to that congregation!

Verify your facts, illustrations and statistics. Yes, it will require additional time, effort, and possibly even research assistance. But it will keep a purity and believability to your message in the long-term.

Confirm that any Scripture you use to prove your point really does prove what you are saying. I remember an outstanding minister pointing this out years ago in a camp meeting. It really registered with me, though I was just a teenage boy of 15. Someone had said that Jesus left 99 sheep "in the fold." The minister pointed out that the Bible did not say that at all. It said that He left 99 sheep "in the wilderness." (See Luke 15:4.) I've heard ministers use quotations from Shakespeare and say that they were in the "Scriptures." They were not. It is very easy to confuse well-known sayings as Scriptures. Confirm them before using them.

When you are uncertain about the material, avoid using it, or announce your uncertainty about the information. Obviously, when you are doing private Bible studies or midweek services, your spontaneity would be too stifled to avoid referencing completely. But, always provide yourself a *verbal disclaimer* by mentioning that "someone told me, though I have not confirmed it." Your feelings are not facts.

Your credibility is inseparable from your believability. It is so important that your people feel comfortable in believing what you are speaking.

Always distinguish to people between something you are feeling, as a man of God, and something God actually spoke to you. Ministers have been known to look at someone and say, "Your husband is coming back home to you. Relax and believe God." Yet, that husband married someone else and never did return to the marriage. It devastated the lady who was hoping the "so-called" prophecy of the minister was correct. The path of Christianity is filled with wounded bodies of hopeful believers who trusted the word of a man of God who simply had a *feeling* about a situation, not a true *word* from God.

Intuition is not the Voice of the Spirit.

The Uncommon Minister must protect the hope of others. Their hope must be in the *Word of God*, not merely the fleeting feelings of the man of God. Pastors are faced with this much more often than traveling ministries. Many pastors have spent hours rebuilding the broken hopes of their people months after a traveling evangelist left who had "a special word from God."

It is obvious you want to be an Uncommon Minister. That's why you're reading this. I urge you to learn the huge difference between your feelings and a true word from God *for* you or *through* you.

Insist On Accuracy In Your Preaching.

It is One of the Secrets of The Uncommon Minister.

⪻ 3 ⪼

LEARN FROM THE UNHAPPY VOICES AROUND YOU.

Unhappy people often birth uncommon ideas.
When you read the biography of great businesses, they always include the complaints of customers. Those complaints created changes, correction and ultimately, uncommon profits. You will often read success suggestions from uncommon entrepreneurs. Every extraordinary business champion states clearly, "Listen to your customers. They will tell you the problems that require solving."

One of the most respected ministers in my life is my dear friend, Sherman Owens, from Sarasota, Florida. I will never forget his teaching: "Listen to happy voices for encouragement. Listen to unhappy voices for *ideas*."

Joseph understood the secret of studying the unhappy. It was the secret of his promotion to the palace. Compassion was his dominant gift. When he noticed the downcast faces of two prisoners, he inquired and pursued an explanation. The butler and baker for Pharaoh explained their dreams. Joseph interpreted those dreams accurately. Two

years later, Joseph was remembered by the butler
for responding to his sorrowful countenance and
dream. Joseph became Prime Minister within 24
hours.

> ▶ You need *encouraging* voices to strengthen
>   you.
> ▶ You need *mentoring* voices to avoid
>   mistakes.
> ▶ You need *unhappy* voices for creativity and
>   ideas.

Listen to the unhappy in your church. People
are rarely angry for the reason they tell you. The
unspoken must be pursued. The unexpressed must
be given time and a season for expression. Take the
time to inquire. Listen without judgment. Permit
others to express their views, fears, and feelings. Was
there a *broken* promise? Unfilled *expectations*? I
still have a deep problem with those who make
promises and continuously alter and change them.

Children find it almost impossible to deal with
the burden of an unkept promise by their parents.

> ▶ Unexpressed disappointment often
>   becomes silent rage.
> ▶ Silent rage often births retaliation and a
>   strategy to destroy.
> ▶ You cannot afford to permit The Unhappy
>   to linger in that condition. Depression,
>   suicide, and even murder has been the
>   result.

Listen to the unhappy on your staff. What is
the real reason for their lack of joy? You Cannot
Solve A Problem That You Do Not See. The doctor
cannot heal a wound he has not discovered. The

lawyer cannot win a case that he does not understand.

Each moment of listening moves you closer to the miracle of solution.

Never assume you understand the real cause of sorrows, despondency, or anger within others. Let me explain. I dearly loved a young couple that worked for me. Continuously, I looked for ways to bless them and encourage them. Occasionally, I would press a large bill in his hand at the airport and say, "Take your wife out to supper tonight." Yet, their agitation persisted. Nothing was ever enough for them. After much thought, listening and study of their life, I discovered the following elements:

► They refused pastoral mentorship and faithful attendance to a local church.
► They refused to follow the principles of success that I taught them privately.
► They refused to attend sessions on financial prosperity held within minutes of their home.

Nothing you can say will satisfy the heart of the disobedient.

Many pastors could have retained and kept disgruntled sheep had they invested the appropriate time to listen long enough to understand them and their pain. On the other hand, many pastors would stop blaming themselves had they understood the deep-rooted problem in unhappy church members.

The best preacher on earth cannot solve the problem of the unteachable. The Unteachable Always Remain Unhappy. That's why Jesus never pursued Pharisees. He never visited them when they were sick. Jesus went where He was desired, not where He was needed.

Do not invest more time in the unhappy than you do those who are supportive and encouraging to you. Too often, those who bless us are ignored. The satisfied are overlooked. The obnoxious often receive far too much time, energy and attention. Be sensitive. That's why Jesus never gave long answers to Pharisees. He saved His time for Zacchaeus and the woman at the well—those who qualified for the Seed of His Attention.

It is not the responsibility of the Uncommon Minister to solve every problem for everyone around him. Jesus did not try. You cannot do it. You are human. Accept that. Do only what you are instructed by the Holy Spirit to do.

Learn From The Unhappy Voices Around You.

It is One of the Secrets of The Uncommon Minister.

≈ 4 ≈

NEVER DISCUSS IN THE PULPIT ANYTHING YOU WANT OTHERS TO FORGET.

Your words are pictures. Unforgettable pictures.

Your words enable thoughts to become permanent. It is dangerous to speak about things that do not really matter. Your words give life and longevity to *anything* discussed.

Words keep many things alive. Many arguments would die; many conflicts would die. But your *words* keep sustaining them.

8 Facts Every Minister Should Know About Words

1. *Words Breathe Life Into Everything.* "Death and life are in the power of the tongue: and they that love it shall eat the fruit thereof" (Proverbs 18:21).

2. *Words Can Wound.* "The words of a talebearer are as wounds, and they go down into the innermost parts of the belly" (Proverbs 18:8).

3. *Words Create Conflict.* "A fools lips enter into contention" (Proverbs 18:6).

4. *Words Can Destroy A Lifetime Friendship In A Moment.* "A froward man soweth strife: and a

whisperer separateth chief friends" (Proverbs 16:28).

5. *Right Words Can Breathe Health Into A Frail Body.* "Pleasant words are as a honeycomb, sweet to the soul, and health to the bones" (Proverbs 16:24). "A wholesome tongue is a tree of life" (Proverbs 15:4).

6. *The Results Of Your Entire Ministry Will Be Impacted By The Words You Select.* "A man hath joy by the answer of his mouth: and a word spoken in due season, how good is it!" (Proverbs 15:23).

7. *Never Stay In The Presence Of People Speaking Wrong Words.* "Go from the presence of a foolish man, when thou perceiveth not in him the lips of knowledge" (Proverbs 14:7).

8. *Any Inappropriate Words You Speak Will Often Be Remembered Longer Than Appropriate Words.* Several years ago, a minister had a devastating experience. False accusations were hurled at him. Emotionally shattered, he shared the experience publicly with some of his congregation. Most of them knew nothing about the false accusations, *until he had brought them out publicly.* It simply created more questions in their mind. Tiny doubts grew like small plants.

"Were they really true after all? Maybe there is another side to the story? Is he telling us *everything*?"

One by one, his supporters dissolved. Yes, the accusations were proven later to be false. But, the damage was done.

He had painted scenarios in their mind that time could not erase. His words were photographs that satan could nurture, feed, and grow *in the privacy of their imagination*.

A pastor in South Louisiana brought me to a beautiful home of a well-known evangelist many years ago. His wife came out and welcomed us warmly. When she disappeared in the back of the house to call for her husband, the pastor turned to me and said, "She was married to a famous baseball manager several years ago. Now, she is married to this evangelist."

I was stunned. When she came back, that thought dominated my mind. She was warm and kind. The conversation was pleasant. But, in the coming days, every time I thought of this evangelist and his wife, I pictured her as married to this famous baseball manager.

A few days later, the pastor and I were driving together again. Suddenly, he said, "Oh, I made a mistake about that wife of the preacher a few days ago. I got her mixed up with someone else. She wasn't married to anyone else before this evangelist."

But *the picture was already in concrete*. That happened 25 years ago, and I am sitting here tonight in my Wisdom Room thinking about this couple. In my mind, she is still married to that baseball manager. The Seed has never quit growing.

You cannot stop everyone from discussing you. But *never provide them information you want them to forget. Nothing*.

Never give unnecessary information that requires, demands, or inspires pursuit of more questions.

Be cautious in confessing all your mistakes. Your

attempts to "be open" may be very sincere. But your mistake may loom bigger *in their memory* than the lesson you are trying to teach from it.

People often remember illustrations for the wrong reasons.

Never Discuss In The Pulpit Something You Want Others To Forget.

It is One of the Secrets of The Uncommon Minister.

❦ 5 ❦

IDENTIFY CONTENTIOUS PEOPLE INVOLVED IN YOUR MINISTRY.

Conflict distracts.

Every minister knows this. When a staff member cannot get along with others, unity and productivity are diminished. Focus is broken. Projects are delayed. The spiritual progress of an entire church can be paralyzed.

Nothing is more harmful to your ministry than a contentious person. A contentious person often considers himself very honest and up front. In fact, they take pride in telling you "the way things really are." Subconsciously, they are often modeling someone in their life (a father or mother) who accomplished their goals through *intimidation.* They admire this person and have decided to follow that pattern. Unfortunately, they failed to see the *losses* created.

13 Facts Every Minister Should Recognize About Contentious People

1. *Contentious People Often Destroy The Momentum, Bonding, And Synergy That Unity*

Creates. "Mark them which cause divisions and offenses...avoid them" (Romans 16:17. See 2 Timothy 2:24 also.)

2. *Contentious People Nullify The Law Of Agreement, The Greatest Law Of Success On Earth.* "Two are better than one; because they have a good reward for their labor. For if they fall, the one will lift up his fellow: but woe unto him that is alone when he falls; for he hath not another to help him up" (Ecclesiastes 4:9,10).

3. *The True Character Of A Contentious Person Is Rarely Revealed Until You Rebuke Them.* If he is a scorner and fool, he will hate you. If he is a wise person simply needing correction, he will love you. "Reprove not a scorner, lest he hate thee: rebuke a wise man, and he will love thee" (Proverbs 9:8).

4. *You Can Succeed Almost Anywhere Else, Except With A Contentious Person.* Solomon experienced this. "It is better to dwell in the corner of the housetop, than with a brawling woman and in a wide house" (Proverbs 25:24).

5. *Contentious People Discuss The Business Of Others.* "He that passeth by, and meddleth with strife belonging not to him, is like one that taketh a dog by the ears" (Proverbs 26:17).

6. *A Contentious Person Enjoys Debate, Disputing And Opposing Whatever Has Been Spoken.* A contentious person always looks for a reason to disagree. They *ignore* every point of *agreement*.

7. *A Contentious Person Is Always The Door For Satan To Launch Every Evil Work In Your Ministry.* "For where envying and strife is, there is confusion and every evil work" (James 3:16).

8. *A Contentious Person Is Not Walking In Wisdom.* "But the Wisdom that is from above is first pure, then peaceable, gentle, and easy to be entreated, full of mercy and good fruits, without partiality, and without hypocrisy" (James 3:17).

9. *A Contentious Attitude Is Contagious.* When someone permits the spirit of conflict to enter their life, they will affect *everyone around them.* I have seen a peaceful household turn to argument 30 minutes after someone entered the room. Happy congregations become chaotic and embittered when one "talebearer" joined the church.

10. *Unthankfulness Always Births A Contentious Attitude.* It is the sin that God abhors. It was the *first* sin. Satan was unthankful for his position and chose to fight for dominion.

11. *Ingratitude Is Poisonous.* It can destroy a family within weeks. It can ruin a successful ministry within months. Churches exploding with growth have been fragmented within weeks when a spirit of ingratitude invaded the congregation.

12. *Contentious People Often Sabotage The Work Of God.* Many years ago I heard one of the most startling statements from a famous missionary. I was sitting under some huge trees in East Africa. Monkeys were jumping from limb to limb.

"Mike, the number one reason missionaries do not stay on the mission field is their *inability to get along with the other missionaries working in their same territory.*"

Think about it. Missionaries who should stay in love with Jesus, obsessed with bringing the gospel to the lost, return home *because of arguments* and the failure to create harmony and an environment of agreement.

13. *Any Contentious Person Who Refuses To Change Must Be Removed.* "Where no wood is, there the fire goeth out: so where there is no talebearer, the strife ceaseth. As coals are to burning coals, and wood to fire; so is a contentious man to kindle strife. The words of a talebearer are as wounds, and they go down into the innermost parts of the belly" (Proverbs 26:20-22).

Stop any conversation birthing contention. Immediately speak up and interrupt the conversation with statements like, "Oh, it is wonderful how God will *turn this* for our good! I am so thankful for what God is about to do in this situation! Don't we have a wonderful God!" It will be like throwing cold water on a destructive fire.

Boldly confront the contentious about their attitude. Others are bold enough to poison your atmosphere and climate with arrows of unthankfulness piercing the air. Dominate your turf. Take charge. Use your words to turn the tide.

Agreement is one of the greatest enemies satan fears.

Identify Contentious People Involved In Your Ministry.

It is One of the Secrets of The Uncommon Minister.

≈ 6 ≈

SECURE THE BEST OFFICE EQUIPMENT POSSIBLE FOR YOUR MINISTRY.

Proper equipment increases your productivity.

I am holding in my hand a microcassette. You see, I can speak six times faster than I can write. If one of my staff was sitting here receiving my dictation, I would be tying up their time for hours. My associate would have to wait for me, time would be wasted and I would feel the pressure of producing and making their moments count. Instead, this microcassette frees them to finish other tasks. Proper machines really help.

Never have someone do a job that a machine can do instead. There are numerous and wonderful reasons for this. Machines cannot think and make judgments in flexible situations. Humans can. So I try to free the time of my staff as much as possible to do those things, and use the machines to do other tasks.

Enjoy these 10 humorous reasons for using proper machines.

10 Reasons To Invest In Quality Equipment

1.   Machines Do Not Require Coaxing, Merely Repair.

2.   Machines Don't Get Discouraged And Disheartened When Their Mother-In-Law Comes To Town.

3.   Machines Are Never Disloyal, Discussing Your Secrets With Everyone Else.

4.   Your Machines Will Not File Grievance Reports Against You With Employment Commissions When You Fail To Meet Their Expectations.

5.   Machines Do Not Require Medical Insurance, Sick Leaves And Time Off.

6.   Machines Can Be Replaced Quickly And Easily.

7.   Machines Do Not Request A Retirement Fund And Want To Be Paid For The Years Ahead When It Cannot Perform.

8.   Machines Never Come To Work Late And Then Ask To Leave Early.

9.   Machines Will Work Through Lunch, Requiring No "Break Time."

10. Machines Never Interrupt The Productivity Of Other Machines When They Are Not Being Used.

This was not my philosophy in my early ministry. In fact, I often refused to purchase expensive equipment. Consequently, it increased the load on my staff. Looking back, this was ludicrous. But, at the time, I felt like it provided work for more staff people. Now, I recognize that people are needed to *supervise* the machines and equipment. This increases their own productivity and worth.

That's why I continuously instruct my staff:

▶ *Find the most effective equipment possible to do your present job.* Telephone other businesses or ministries. Attend seminars and workshops. Whatever it takes to do your job more efficiently, more accurately and quickly—tell me. I will do anything possible to make the hours of my employees more effective and productive.

▶ *Continuously evaluate your productivity.* What is slowing you down? What machine could make a big difference in the completion of your daily tasks and responsibilities?

▶ *Present me with options to your present equipment.*

When you become computer-minded, equipment oriented and aware of the remarkable inventions of our day, you will increase the productivity of your ministry dramatically. Your staff will treasure it and learn to appreciate their own work load reduction because of it. It decreases their opportunities for mistakes. It increases the standardization of their work.

Secure The Best Office Equipment Possible For Your Ministry.

It is One of the Secrets of The Uncommon Minister.

⚘ 7 ⚘

VALUE THE VOWS OF YOUR PEOPLE.

⚞━━⯈●⯇━━

Vows matter greatly to God.
Vows are not playful moments.
Vows are the catalyst for miracles. "When thou vowest a vow to God, defer not to pay it; for He hath no pleasure in fools: pay that which thou hast vowed. Better is it that thou shouldest not vow than thou shouldest vow and not pay" (Ecclesiastes 5:4,5).
Promise Breakers are *fools.*
Promise Makers are *wise.*
Promise Keepers are *rewarded.* Always.

4 Facts Every Minister Should Know About Vows And Covenants

1. *God Is A Covenant God.* He makes agreements and contracts with those who honor His integrity.

2. *Uncommon Champions Often Make Uncommon Vows To God.* One of the most effective mentors ever, Dr. Lester Sumrall, made a vow to God. He believed that he would die unless he kept that vow. He told God that if He would heal him, he would preach this gospel the rest of his life. He kept that vow and blessed millions. God always

guarantees blessings to those who observe and "do all His commandments" (see Deuteronomy 28:1).

3.   *Vows Will Often Emerge During The Season Of A Special Anointing Or Challenge Of Faith By A Man Of God.*   I was sitting at the table with Oral Roberts.   Suddenly, the Holy Spirit rose up strong for me to sow an unforgettable and uncommon Seed into his life. Why? The anointing upon him was the *magnet* that unleashed my own faith.

While sitting in a conference, a man of God challenged the ministers present to plant an unusual Seed.   My heart leaped. I sowed the Seed and experienced an incredible encounter with the Holy Spirit less than 30 days later.

4.   *Encourage Your People To Keep Their Vows To The Work Of God.*   Don't be discouraged when many vows are not kept. Everyone requires teaching. Everyone becomes discouraged.

Recently, a pastor friend lamented the lack of follow through on the faith promises of people. He was agitated and almost critical.

"Many of my people are not completing their faith promises. Thousands of dollars are promised to the work of God, and they are not completing these vows."

I inquired, "Think for a moment. What did you do following the service when they came forward to the altar and made those faith promises?"

Total silence. He had done *nothing.* I explained patiently to him that when anyone comes into the presence of God, their faith will ignite. Hope leaps. Doubt evaporates. When your people come into the presence of God, they receive *glimpses* of their next season. They are ecstatic, stirred and excited. Remember, when the Israelites received an inward photograph of Canaan, their energy exploded. Life becomes exciting because of the *dominant* picture in your heart.

"When your people left the church service, that anointing received an attack," I explained. "They entered the world of their business, television reports and relatives who voiced doubt, sarcasm and even unbelief. Their faith always takes a beating following their step toward God."

He was puzzled but I continued. "When your people make faith promises, they are reacting to the supernatural presence of God. The Holy Spirit has spoken to their heart. They respond to His voice with acts of faith. But when they return to their homes, the climate changes. The atmosphere becomes adversarial. Their families bicker, quarrel, and even become angry over their step of faith. Many of your people endure sarcastic words from relatives about the church, prosperity preachers, and televangelists."

I encouraged him to remember this and *value the vows of his people.*

It is One of the Secrets of the Uncommon Minister.

Complete your personal library of
"The Uncommon Minister" Series. These first seven
volumes are a must for your ministry reading.
Practical and powerful, these Wisdom Keys will
enhance your ministry expression for years to come.

ITEM	TITLE	QTY	PRICE	TOTAL
B107	The Uncommon Minister, Volume 1		$5.00	$
B108	The Uncommon Minister, Volume 2		$5.00	$
B109	The Uncommon Minister, Volume 3		$5.00	$
B110	The Uncommon Minister, Volume 4		$5.00	$
B111	The Uncommon Minister, Volume 5		$5.00	$
B112	The Uncommon Minister, Volume 6		$5.00	$
B113	The Uncommon Minister, Volume 7		$5.00	$
All 7 Volumes of The Uncommon Minister			$35.00	$

Mail To: **The Wisdom Center** P.O. Box 99 Denton, TX 76202 940-891-1400	Add 10% For Shipping	$
	(Canada add 20% to retail cost and 20% shipping)	$
	Enclosed Is My Seed-Faith Gift For Your Ministry	$
	Total Amount Enclosed	$

SORRY NO C.O.D.'S

Name _____
Address _____
City _____
State _____
Zip _____   Telephone _____

❑ Check ❑ Money Order
❑ Visa   ❑ Master Card ❑ Amex

Signature _____
Exp. Date _____
Card No. _____

THE
WISDOM
CENTER

—— Quantity Prices for ——
"The Uncommon Minister" Series

1-9	=	$5.00 each
10-99	=	$4.00 each (20% discount)
100-499	=	$3.50 each (30% discount)
500-999	=	$3.00 each (40% discount)
1,000-up	=	$2.50 each (50% discount)
5,000-up	=	$2.00 each (60% discount)

POWERFUL WISDOM BOOKS FROM DR. MIKE MURDOCK!

You can increase your Wisdom Library by purchasing any one of these great titles by *MIKE MURDOCK*. Scriptural, practical, readable. These books are life-changing!

The Covenant Of 58 Blessings

Dr. Murdock shares the phenomenon of the 58 Blessings, his experiences, testimonials, and the words of God Himself concerning the 58 Blessings. Your life will never be the same! (Paperback)
(B47) 86 pages $8

The Proverbs 31 Woman

God's ultimate woman is described in Proverbs 31. *Dr. Murdock* breaks it down to the pure revelation of these 31 marvelous qualities. (Paperback)
(B49) 68 pages $7

Wisdom - God's Golden Key To Success

In this book, *Dr. Mike Murdock* shares his insight into the Wisdom of God that will remove the veil of ignorance and propel you into the abundant life. (Paperback)
(B70) 67 pages $7

Secrets Of The Richest Man Who Ever Lived

This teaching on the life of Solomon will bring you to a higher level of understanding in the 31 secrets of uncommon wealth and success. God's best will soon be yours as you learn and put into practice these keys. (Paperback)
(B99) 192 pages $10

Remember...God sent His Son, but He left His Book!

Wisdom For Crisis Times

Discover the Wisdom Keys to dealing with tragedies, stress and times of crisis. Secrets that will unlock the answers in the right way to react in life situations. (Paperback)
(B40) 118 pages $9

The Double Diamond Principle

This explosive book contains 58 Master Secrets for Total Success in the life of Jesus that will help you achieve your goals and dreams. (Paperback)
(B39) 144 pages $9

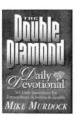

The Double Diamond Daily Devotional

This devotional for every day of the year is filled with dynamic Wisdom keys and Scriptures for successful leaders and achievers. This volume includes topics on dreams and goals, relationships, miracles, prosperity and more!
(Paperback)
(B80) 374 pages $12

Wisdom For Winning

The best-selling handbook for achieving success. Every obstacle and pitfall to abundant success is covered in this powerful volume. This book will put you in the "Winner's World." If you desire to be successful and happy, this is the book for you! (Paperback)
(B01) 220 pages $10

Thirty-One Secrets Of An Unforgettable Woman

Dynamic Wisdom Keys to unveil secrets of one of the greatest Biblical women in history, Ruth. This book will change you! (Paperback)
(B57) Over 130 pages $9

Dream Seeds

What do you dream of doing with your life? What would you attempt to do if you knew it was impossible to fail? This 118 page book helps you answer these questions and much more! (Paperback)
(B11) 118 pages $9

ORDER FORM THE MIKE MURDOCK WISDOM LIBRARY

(All books paperback unless indicated otherwise.)

QTY	CODE	BOOK TITLE	USA	TOTAL
	B01	WISDOM FOR WINNING	$10	
	B02	5 STEPS OUT OF DEPRESSION	$ 2	
	B03	THE SEX TRAP	$ 2	
	B04	10 LIES PEOPLE BELIEVE ABOUT MONEY	$ 2	
	B05	FINDING YOUR PURPOSE IN LIFE	$ 2	
	B06	CREATING TOMORROW THROUGH SEED-FAITH	$ 2	
	B07	BATTLE TECHNIQUES FOR WAR WEARY SAINTS	$ 2	
	B08	ENJOYING THE WINNING LIFE	$ 2	
	B09	FOUR FORCES/GUARANTEE CAREER SUCCESS	$ 2	
	B10	THE BRIDGE CALLED DIVORCE	$ 2	
	B11	DREAM SEEDS	$ 9	
	B12	YOUNG MINISTERS HANDBOOK	$20	
	B13	SEEDS OF WISDOM ON DREAMS AND GOALS	$ 3	
	B14	SEEDS OF WISDOM ON RELATIONSHIPS	$ 3	
	B15	SEEDS OF WISDOM ON MIRACLES	$ 3	
	B16	SEEDS OF WISDOM ON SEED-FAITH	$ 3	
	B17	SEEDS OF WISDOM ON OVERCOMING	$ 3	
	B18	SEEDS OF WISDOM ON HABITS	$ 3	
	B19	SEEDS OF WISDOM ON WARFARE	$ 3	
	B20	SEEDS OF WISDOM ON OBEDIENCE	$ 3	
	B21	SEEDS OF WISDOM ON ADVERSITY	$ 3	
	B22	SEEDS OF WISDOM ON PROSPERITY	$ 3	
	B23	SEEDS OF WISDOM ON PRAYER	$ 3	
	B24	SEEDS OF WISDOM ON FAITH TALK	$ 3	
	B25	SEEDS OF WISDOM ONE YEAR DEVOTIONAL	$10	
	B26	THE GOD BOOK	$10	
	B27	THE JESUS BOOK	$10	
	B28	THE BLESSING BIBLE	$10	
	B29	THE SURVIVAL BIBLE	$10	
	B30	TEENAGERS TOPICAL BIBLE	$ 6	
	B30L	TEENAGERS TOPICAL BIBLE (LEATHER)	$20	
	B31	ONE-MINUTE TOPICAL BIBLE	$12	
	B32	MINISTER'S TOPICAL BIBLE	$ 6	
	B33	BUSINESSMAN'S TOPICAL BIBLE	$ 6	
	B33L	BUSINESSMAN'S TOPICAL BIBLE (LEATHER)	$20	
	B34L	GRANDPARENT'S TOPICAL BIBLE (LEATHER)	$20	
	B35	FATHER'S TOPICAL BIBLE	$ 6	
	B35L	FATHER'S TOPICAL BIBLE (LEATHER)	$20	
	B36	MOTHER'S TOPICAL BIBLE	$ 6	
	B36L	MOTHER'S TOPICAL BIBLE (LEATHER)	$20	
	B37	NEW CONVERT'S BIBLE	$ 6	
	B38	THE WIDOW'S TOPICAL BIBLE	$ 6	
	B39	THE DOUBLE DIAMOND PRINCIPLE	$ 9	
	B40	WISDOM FOR CRISIS TIMES	$ 9	
	B41	THE GIFT OF WISDOM (VOLUME ONE)	$ 8	
	B42	ONE-MINUTE BUSINESSMAN'S DEVOTIONAL	$10	
	B43	ONE-MINUTE BUSINESSWOMAN'S DEVOTIONAL	$10	
	B44	31 SECRETS FOR CAREER SUCCESS	$10	
	B45	101 WISDOM KEYS	$ 7	
	B46	31 FACTS ABOUT WISDOM	$ 7	
	B47	THE COVENANT OF 58 BLESSINGS	$ 8	
	B48	31 KEYS TO A NEW BEGINNING	$ 7	
	B49	31 SECRETS OF THE PROVERBS 31 WOMAN	$ 7	
	B50	ONE-MINUTE POCKET BIBLE FOR ACHIEVERS	$ 5	
	B51	ONE-MINUTE POCKET BIBLE FOR FATHERS	$ 5	
	B52	ONE-MINUTE POCKET BIBLE FOR MOTHERS	$ 5	

Mail to: Dr. Mike Murdock • The Wisdom Training Center • P.O. Box 99 • Denton, TX 76202
(940) 891-1400 Or USA Call Toll Free **1-888-WISDOM-1**

Qty	Code	Book Title	USA	Total
	B53	One-Minute Pocket Bible For Teenagers	$ 5	
	B54	One-Minute Daily Devotional(hardback)	$14	
	B55	20 Keys To A Happier Marriage	$ 2	
	B56	How To Turn Mistakes To Miracles	$ 2	
	B57	31 Secrets Of The Unforgettable Woman	$ 9	
	B58	Mentor's Manna On Attitude	$ 2	
	B59	The Making Of A Champion	$ 6	
	B60	One-Minute Pocket Bible For Men	$ 5	
	B61	One-Minute Pocket Bible For Women	$ 5	
	B62	One-Minute Pocket Bible For Bus. Professionals	$ 5	
	B63	One-Minute Pocket Bible For Truckers	$ 5	
	B64	Mentor's Manna On Achievement	$ 2	
	B65	Mentor's Manna On Adversity	$ 2	
	B66	Greed, Gold And Giving	$ 2	
	B67	Gift Of Wisdom For Champions	$ 8	
	B68	Gift Of Wisdom For Achievers	$ 8	
	B69	Mentor's Manna on The Secret Place	$ 2	
	B70	Gift Of Wisdom For Mothers	$ 8	
	B71	Wisdom-God's Golden Key To Success	$ 7	
	B72	The Double Diamond Daily Devotional	$12	
	B73	Mentor's Manna On Abilities	$ 2	
	B74	The Assignment: Dream/Destiny #1	$10	
	B75	The Assignment: Anointing/Adversity #2	$10	
	B76	The Assignment: Trials/Triumphs #3	$10	
	B77	The Assignment: Pain/Passion #4	$10	
	B78	Wisdom Keys For A Powerful Prayer Life	$ 2	
	B79	7 Obstacles To Abundant Success	$ 2	
	B80	The Greatest Success Habit On Earth	$ 2	
	B81	Born To Taste The Grapes	$ 2	
	B82	31 Reasons People Do Not Receive Their Financial Harvest	$12	
	B83	Gift Of Wisdom For Wives	$ 8	
	B84	Gift Of Wisdom For Husbands	$ 8	
	B85	Gift Of Wisdom For Teenagers	$ 8	
	B86	Gift Of Wisdom For Leaders	$ 8	
	B87	Gift Of Wisdom For Graduates	$ 8	
	B88	Gift Of Wisdom For Brides	$ 8	
	B89	Gift Of Wisdom For Grooms	$ 8	
	B90	Gift Of Wisdom For Ministers	$ 8	
	B91	The Leadership Secrets Of Jesus(hdbk)	$15	
	B92	Secrets Of The Journey (Vol. 1)	$ 5	
	B93	Secrets Of The Journey (Vol. 2)	$ 5	
	B94	Secrets Of The Journey (Vol. 3)	$ 5	
	B95	Secrets Of The Journey (Vol. 4)	$ 5	

☐ CASH ☐ CHECK ☐ MONEY ORDER

☐ VISA ☐ MASTER CARD ☐ AMEX

CREDIT CARD #

EXPIRATION DATE [ ][ ][ ][ ] *SORRY NO C.O.D.'s*

SIGNATURE _____

TOTAL PAGE 2	$
TOTAL PAGE 1	$
*ADD SHIPPING 10% USA / 20% OTHERS	$
CANADA CURRENCY DIFFERENCE ADD 20%	$
TOTAL ENCLOSED	$

PLEASE PRINT

Name _____

Address _____

City _____

State _____ Zip _____

Phone ( ) _____

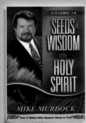

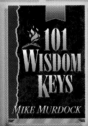

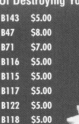

The Secret To 1000 Times More.

In this Dynamic Video you will find answers to unleash Financial Flow into your life!

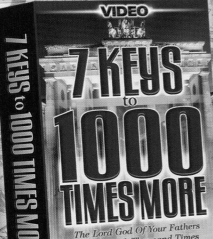

- ▶ Habits Of Uncommon Achievers
- ▶ The Greatest Success Law I Ever Discovered
- ▶ How To Discern Your Place Of Assignment, The Only Place Financial Provision Is Guaranteed
- ▶ 3 Secret Keys In Solving Problems For Others
- ▶ How To Become The Next Person To Receive A Raise On Your Job

Wisdom Is The Principal Thing

Video VI-16 / $30
Six Audio Tapes / $30 TS-77
Book / $10 B-104

The Wisdom Center

Somebody's Future Will Not Begin Until You Enter.

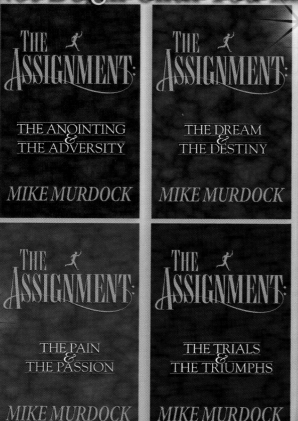

THIS COLLECTION INCLUDES 4 DIFFERENT BOOKS CONTAINING UNCOMMON WISDOM FOR DISCOVERING YOUR LIFE ASSIGNMENT

▶ How To Achieve A God-Given Dream And Goal

▶ How To Know Who Is Assigned To You

▶ The Purpose And Rewards Of An Enemy

Wisdom Is The Principal Thing
Book Pak
WBL-14 / **$30**
Buy 3-Get 1 Free
($10 Each/$40 Value!)
The Wisdom Center

The Secret Place
Library Pak

Songs from the Secret Place

Over 40 Great Songs On 6 Music Tapes
Including "I'm In Love" / Love Songs From The Holy Spirit
Birthed In The Secret Place / <u>Side A</u> Is Dr. Mike Murdock
Singing / <u>Side B</u> Is Music Only For Your Personal Prayer Time

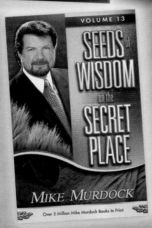

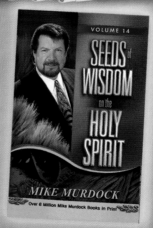

Seeds of Wisdom on the Secret Place

4 Secrets The Holy Spirit Reveals In The Secret Place / The Necessary
Ingredients In Creating Your Secret Place / 10 Miracles That Will
Happen In The Secret Place

Seeds of Wisdom on the Holy Spirit

The Protocol For Entering The Presence Of
The Holy Spirit / the greatest day of my life and
What Made It So / Power Keys For Developing Your
Personal Relationship With The Holy Spirit

Wisdom Is The Principal Thing
Book/Tape Pak
SP PAK-001 / **$30**
Six Audio Tapes & Two Books
(A $40 Value!)
The Wisdom Center

The SCHOOL of WISDOM

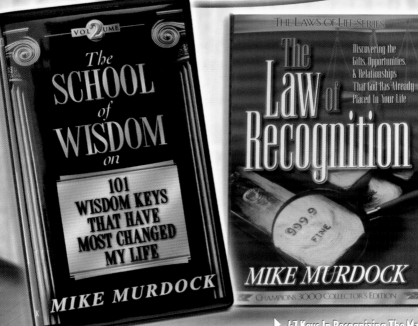

THE LAWS OF LIFE SERIES

The Law of Recognition

Discovering the Gifts, Opportunities, & Relationships That God Has Already Placed In Your Life

VOLUME 2

The SCHOOL of WISDOM on

101 WISDOM KEYS THAT HAVE MOST CHANGED MY LIFE

MIKE MURDOCK

CHAMPIONS 3000 COLLECTOR'S EDITION

▶ 47 Keys In Recognizing The Mate God Has Approved For You

▶ 14 Facts You Should Know About Your Gifts and Talents

▶ 17 Important Facts You Should Remember About Your Weakness

▶ And Much, Much More...

▶ What Attracts Others Toward You

▶ The Secret Of Multiplying Your Financial Blessings

▶ What Stops The Flow Of Your Faith

▶ Why Some Fail And Others Succeed

▶ How To Discern Your Life Assignment

▶ How To Create Currents Of Favor With Others

▶ How To Defeat Loneliness

Wisdom Is The Principal Thing

Book/Tape Pak / $30
PAK-002
Six Audio Tapes & Book
(A $40 Value!)

The Wisdom Center

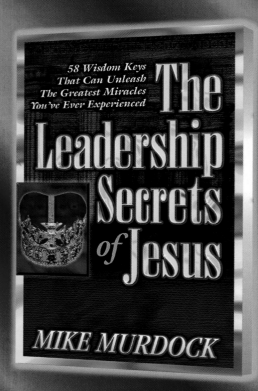

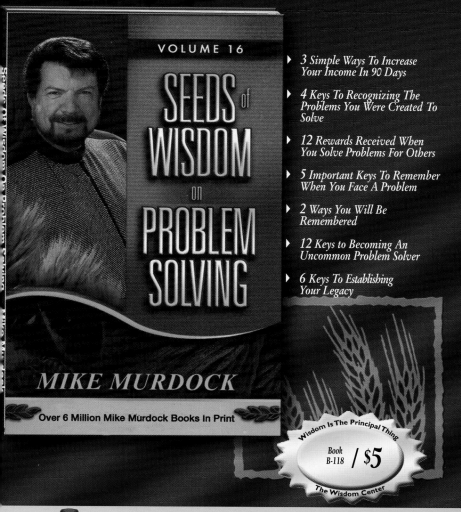

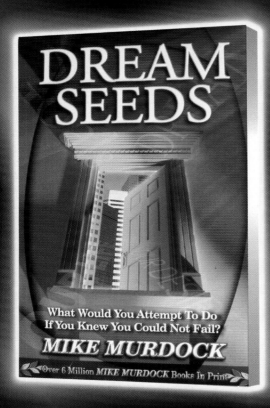

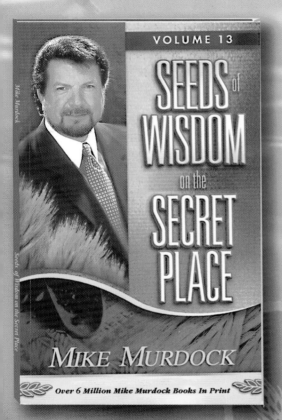

Run To Win.

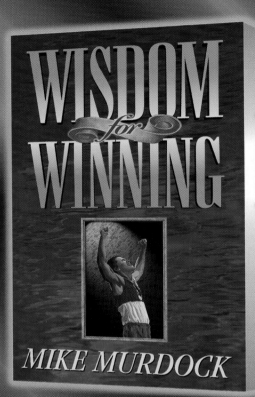

- 10 Ingredients For Success
- Ten Lies Many People Believe About Money
- 20 Keys For Winning At Work
- 20 Keys To A Better Marriage
- 3 Facts Every Parent Should Remember
- 5 Steps Out Of Depression
- The Greatest Wisdom Principle I Ever Learned
- 7 Keys To Answered Prayer
- God's Master Golden Key To Total Success
- The Key To Understanding Life

Everyone needs to feel they have achieved something with their life. When we stop producing, loneliness and laziness will choke all enthusiasm from our living. What would you like to be doing? What are you doing about it? Get started on a project in your life. Start building on your dreams. Resist those who would control and change your personal goals. Get going with this powerful teaching and reach your life goals!

Wisdom Is The Principal Thing

Book B-01 / $10

Six Audio Tapes TS-01 / $30

The Wisdom Center

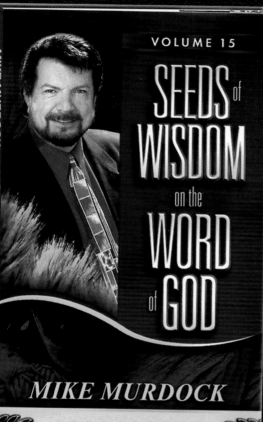

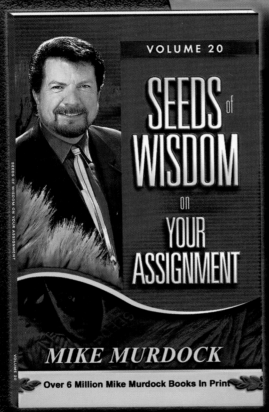

WISDOM COLLECTION

SECRETS OF THE UNCOMMON MILLIONAIRE

1. **The Uncommon Millionaire Conference Vol. 1 (Six Cassettes)**
2. **The Uncommon Millionaire Conference Vol. 2 (Six Cassettes)**
3. **The Uncommon Millionaire Conference Vol. 3 (Six Cassettes)**
4. **The Uncommon Millionaire Conference Vol. 4 (Six Cassettes)**
5. **31 Reasons People Do Not Receive Their Financial Harvest (256 Page Book)**
6. **Secrets of the Richest Man Who Ever Lived (178 Page Book)**
7. **12 Seeds of Wisdom Books On 12 Topics**
8. **The Gift of Wisdom for Leaders Desk Calendar**
9. **Songs From The Secret Place (Music Cassette)**
10. **In Honor of the Holy Spirit (Music Cassette)**
11. **365 Memorization Scriptures On The Word Of God (Audio Cassette)**

Wisdom Is The Principal Thing
THE WISDOM COLLECTION 8
SECRETS OF THE UNCOMMON
MILLIONAIRE
WC-08 /$195
The Wisdom Center